A Complicated Relationship with Fire

War and Other Unpleasant Legal Matters

D.R. Dunne

Acknowledgments

I dedicate this book to my children; first my daughter Lillith because she's pretty sure I don't care as much for her as I do for the others, which simply isn't the case. Then, in no particular order Evan, Daniel and Thomas, and my step-children Isabel, Gabriel and Abigail. You seven are the loves of my life, and everything that makes it worthwhile. I miss you all without end, and look forward to the day we all can sit together, meet, and catch up.

To my husband Steven for sticking by me no matter what, and to Paul for fucking it up heavily enough that I had to sprout wings on my own. To Chris for NOT giving in to peer pressure back in the SAC. To Lewey for being my pretend Dad when my real Father went nuts. To the old MRF crew, thank you and love to you all.

To my brothers and sisters at Convocation and Pagan Pathways Temple, to George, Cat, Mac, "Selena" (Zeinab), Emilie and the old RDV crew, who always told me I could do this, and to the rest of my family for being a constant source of inspiration.

Some of these poems are based in my own personal truths, some are not. I challenge you to find the difference, for in human experience, we are one, and our pain is mirrored on each other's' faces.

My story is sprawled out on these pages between my leftist drivel and my innermost fears. I lived this. My daughter really was molested, I really did encourage my own ex-husband to turn himself in, and I really did have the cops meet me at Exit 1 on the Michigan border to make it all happen. I really haven't seen my birth sons in 4 years, I really did call the ACLU, and they really couldn't help me, my Father really didn't allow me time alone with him in the days before his death. The rest are just tidbits from the time at the tone, (which is now) and in the time before, (pre-2013, when the molestation was discovered and acted upon) and in the time after, (any time after that.)

When forces so deeply dark close in on you, it takes a village to pull you up. I had, (and still have) a mighty village. I am grateful to every single one of you, you have all taught me something. I love you, I have faith in you, and please enjoy my madness.

Contents

The Time at the Tone is Now

Altruism

I am my Father's Daughter
I was doomed to become
This person that I see now
In the sky's mirror

I am my Mother's Daughter
And so I was doomed to become
Nurturer, lover protector and noose.

I've got a coffee in one hand and a roving eye in
my head
I have a quick wit and dispense hidden insults with
poise and confidence
When I look in the mirror I will always be too fat for
my liking
When I look in the mirror I will always be too bald
When I look at my heart, I will have to evaluate
Whether or not I am helping for my own selfish
gain or out of true altruism.

Bidding on Death

I'm hurt
And there isn't money
To pay for my medications
Or the surgery i need to stay alive
Or the therapy i'll need to unplant these scars
From the PTSD
I suffer now
Thanks
To some asshole
Who needed to show me
Who was boss

My only choice is to beg
And i will beg
And beg until i can no longer beg
And people will criticize me
For buying avocados
And bread
And the foods that
Keep me alive
Because i do not deserve to eat
Anything but pink slime
Forever

And ever
Amen

They don't care, you know
Unless you are unborn
Or related to them in some way
And you can't make them care
You can't reason with the unreasonable
On either side of the equation
They see it just
As impossible
To forgive my choice
To abort an embryo
Who is holding my body hostage
Under the body share program
If i carry to term i am a teenage Mom
And people lose all respect for me
If i don't, they call me a murderer
And maybe they should
But that seems like a question for a higher power
Who may or may not exist
And a question for when i am on my deathbed

Oh wait
I am on my deathbed
Right, i forgot

So bid on my life
Or my death
Maybe you could have my eyes when i die
Shiny brown orbs of regret
Or my cunt
Or my eczema scarred skin
Or my defective nerves
My half dead heart
Or how about that atypical brain of mine?

Up for sale
Selling my body to the highest bidder
I am not above offering a blowjob if it means I get
to live
Hell, shit on my face
Make me eat myself out at gunpoint
Because
What the hell else
Do i have to give to prove
My life is worth
The same as the unborn fertilized egg
I used to carry in my womb

Dream

I dream of a world where

An autistic woman can raise her children
After putting her pedophile ex-husband in jail
And not be ostracized from her group of friends
And not be ostracized by the school system she
sought out for help
And not be ostracized by the people she called
family.

I dream
That this isn't too much to ask
And that my request, although unconventional
Be considered
And given as much weight
As a Nazi rally
By the press
And the ACLU
And by the president
And have it seen by everyone
As the crime that it is

I dream of a world where

Said pedophile could have gotten help
Before he abused a child

I dream
Of a world where
My daughter wasn't afraid to call out a rapist
And where
She felt she had the ability to
Say no
To her captors
And to say no to anyone
Except herself.
She should be able to say yes to herself anytime
the mood strikes
Twice, and then twice more
YES.
I am worthy
I am loved
I deserve to further my education
I deserve to be loved and taken care of
By my human family

Yes
But those dreams are just dreams
Until a time when things change,

Change is a funny word
That evokes such fear into the shortsighted
Like, for a second believe the world
Doesn't have to be filled to the brim with racists
And bigots
And classists

I dream
Of a world where my brothers and sisters
Of another color skin can speak of their pain
And see it reflected in the eyes of others
Where people can be present with them
And commiserate
And apologize
And honestly mean what they say
And be heard for what they say

Sometimes
All we can do is
Act like cats through the window frame
Never speaking a word
But staring into the eyes of another and
Through them
Know their entire world

At a glance.

These are but lofty dreams
Of a dreamer
A Granddaughter of immigrants
A shining sea away
From the world they once knew

hey.

how've things been since you ruined our lives?

i've been pretty busy cleaning up your messes

and

dealing with the fact

that your parents hate me for having you locked

up

and

the mourning i feel for

my daughter

who will never know a normal loving relationship

so thanks for that.

hey

how's the coffee and the conversation

there

behind the metal walls guarded by gun towers

how does it feel to look at barbed wires

for the rest of your life.

hey

you raped her.

you admitted this to the cops, random friends of

the family, me…

why won't you fess up to your parents

because they do not believe the 2 separate trials

you have stood accused

apparently weren't enough to convince them

that this wasn't some witchy trick i pulled

with my crystals and my karma

and who the fuck cares really?

i make my days the same way that some people

breathe

with intention, and thought, and every day it is a

struggle just to

get out of bed

put on my clothes

head out the door to a job that i hate

every day is a struggle to

convince my daughter of her beauty

convince my daughter she needs therapy

because even if it doesn't hurt now

it will later

it'll come up like an unresolved chord progression

in a song

like a bubbling sewage system

like the death of a loved one

or a song that won't escape your mind

this is the song that never ends

about molestation, and rape, and abuse

and how mama got fooled

and now, the babies are with the folks who

raised a pedophile

because, at the time, when presented with the

choices between

going with strangers, going with my family or

going with yours

they seemed like the best equipped to handle it

because of the money

it was always due to the money.

hey.

every day i must remind her

that her brothers being at your parents house is

not her fault

that she not seeing them for the past 4 years isn't

her fault

but it's yours

and so conditioned she was since the age of 6

that she is convinced

that she should have kept quiet

and just endured your violations

til the end of time so that i could raise she and her

brothers

hey

you could fix this, but you won't.

you just have to tell your parents

tell them about our open marriage

and about how you had no impulse control

about how you took advantage of a 6 year old

and just kept doing it again and again

and

pretend that there is something normal about that

not vile

but you won't.

i will never see our sons again

because

i didn't have the strength to stand before the court

as the accused

because i was told that, i would never win

that i was flawed

because of my autism

and that i would never see the world around me

for what it was

full of apples that were full of razor blades

and i understand now

that the apples and razors resided under my

kitchen sink this whole time

hey

you could fix this

i have tried and failed

she could fix this, and she has tried and failed

no one can fix this

and here i am, for the fourth consecutive year

with my head

in my hands

meanwhile trying to steal a glance at

the children i gave birth to

in our apartment, with midwives

and we were so very excited

and so relieved

and they grew into savants who were good at

sports

and enjoyed volunteering at food banks

and read at a post high school level in elementary

school

stolen

because my spectrum diagnosis

and because i would never amount to much

hey

someone fix this please

i am drowning

but i refused to play the victim for so long now

that i don't know what playing the victim looks like

i'm lost

Help Me.

Long may you grow

When I turned away
I had to leave
It wasn't what I wanted,
Or what I had hoped to achieve
But it was for the best
My greatest test
I hope that you'd be proud of me
And that I could say the same

Long may you grow
Long may you shine
Your lives will always be an echo of mine
Long may you grow
And may you see
The truth that is surrounding us
Can you please forgive me

When I stayed away
Know that I was chased
Never would have willingly
Wandered off base
I told the truth
May you believe

Whatever path you wish to tread
I'm sure you will see

Long may you grow
Long may you shine
Your lives will always be an echo of mine
Long may you grow
And may you see
The path that is surrounding you
May it be what you need

Long may you grow
(Grow strong near the babbling brook)
Long may you shine
(Grow strong like the black walnut)
Your lives will always be an echo of mine

Long may you grow
(As you spread your wings to find me)
And may you see
(Missing you forever)
The path that is surrounding you
(Find me as you spread your wings)
May it be what you need

Make your own days

You had one night
To make it all right
But instead you threw it all away
You wasted your life
On a child in sunshine
And there are no words for your mistake

It doesn't get easier, you know
The ice cream just gets sweeter
When you learn to make your own days
All the little moments, you know
Just go on as you go
And you wish that you could turn back time
But it doesn't get easier
It just fades

You had one day
To make it go away
But instead, you argued with the judge
You wasted your chance
On a child's first dance
And I wondered if I was about to break

It doesn't get easier, you know
The ice cream just gets sweeter
When you learn to make your own days
All the little moments, you know
Just go on as you go
And you wish that you could turn back time
But it doesn't get easier
It just fades

You had one chance
To put this in the past

But instead, you cowered in your cell
You could have been honest
And cleared your conscious
But instead you let the whole thing go

We were depending on you
You were our only hope
And instead, you put your ego first
It doesn't get easier at all
The time just goes deeper until
The memories show and then...
They just fade.

Mental illness is fatal if swallowed

Nursing killed my father

Video killed the radio star

Co-Dependence killed my father

Compliance killed the leftist movement

And i murdered hope

We're all the same, right?

Same same, eye for another stupid eye?

I wish i had eyes that shined like the galaxy

Blue, purple and white on a vast cloud of murky
black

His eyes were nebulae

And he said he would help me

Offered a hand

Instead of a dick pic

Offered kind words

Instead of another harsh criticism

When i was at my lowest,
I was alone
And hungry
At the bottom
Of a well
Looking upward
Clawing frantically at the edges
Of the well
I dug
Of my own hand
And at the top i found
I hadn't missed a whole lot of living

Things I did miss?
Being able to be complacent
Without my whole world tumbling down.
As it turns out
The whole world can turn on you
If you're a slut
And it's ok.

My dad didn't come to save me
He didn't even offer me
Time alone with him in a room
Before his grand exit.
Had to have his toothless old hag there

Cursing to her back, but never to her face and i
Sought the truth
And found only my father
Laying in a bed
Blood cooling
Whore making a production out of mourning
Which would have won an Emmy
If… she didn't suck at it.

Her children
Taking selfies with my father's corpse
And my daughter
Stringently yelling in such a way
I have never heard
With a strength she didn't know she possessed.
Closing the room off to mourners

My sister
Drinking coffee
As though it was a normal thing for her to do.
She always hated coffee
My uncle
Brought to his knees
And the dachshunds
Following all the doggy stages of grief.
And removing what from the house we could

Before the whore came in
And she did
Against my advice
And gutted the place clean

These are just things
No man lived here
Just a shell
Of a father figure
With a lifetime of regret to
Figure out

My hand is empty

It was a beautiful day today,

the sun was shining,
70 degrees,
perfect for a late fall evening.
My hand was empty though.

There was no one there to hold it.
I walked along the river's edge,
noting the rose petals,
shaped like hearts, that lined the boat dock.
When I looked up that hill,
I saw you there, towering, Daniel on your
shoulders,
Evan running beside you.
You in your work uniform,
and I felt the fatigue of the baby I was carrying.
It was a flashback, of course, but all too vivid.

My hand is empty.

Your promise of forever as empty as my hand.
You promised me you,
you promised me the kids,

and my hand is empty.

You promised me a trip to Scotland, and to Ireland.
 You promised me a new dress, you promised me
a replacement wedding ring but… My hand is still
empty.

How could you?
How could you leave my hand empty?
How could you think my daughter's hand was a
suitable replacement?
We were in an open marriage, you could have had
ANY woman or man you wanted,
and you chose one of the 4 people in the world
who were completely off limits to you.
But right now, at this very moment, this isn't about
them.
I cannot say how my daughter is feeling, how my
sons are, because my own hand is empty.
I feel only the emptiness of my own hand.

I cannot process this empty hand.
We were a FAMILY,
I drove a huge SUV down the dirt roads with
reckless abandon,

my hand was not empty then!
You were there, hand in mine, thin, long fingers
interlaced.
A gentle smile on your face, sympathetic eyes
shining.

PITY!
IT WAS PITY.
Pity isn't love.
This,
just as every other thing I have fucking lived in the
past 4 years, has been a lie.
The only thing real from that time was that our son
was born.
Held the sweet baby in my arms while
he was still covered in my blood, smelled his smell,

kissed his tiny forehead
and breastfed him
while I delivered the placenta in our small
bedroom.
And you cut the cord.

A son is a promise to a mother that there will be
someone to hold her hand forever.
And yet, my hand is EMPTY.

My hands held his hand while he fed,
while I changed his diapers,
while he learned to crawl,
and to walk,
And every night while he fell asleep
And he was my promise that, no matter what happened
I would be ok.

You
Cut
The
Cord

My hand is, and shall remain always
Empty.

When it should have been so full
That the world marveled
At the beauty that was too beautiful
And the lie that was
Too good
To be
True.

My heart:

No Trespassing

No

Soliciting

Signposts and Measures

You are here

And here is good
It is quantitative
Measurable
Palatable

If you keep reaching
There will eventually be good
But there are some evil things that lurk
In the corners of your psyche
And some dark overpasses
In the highway of your mind

But there are no signposts
No GPS to say "you are here" and
Here is good
I just feel like I'm ready now
Ready to see my kids and face their new parents
but
I am not allowed
The universe will not allow it.

I don't understand what I did

In all of those measures years ago
That convinced someone that grand trickery was
involved
Haven't I always been honest to more than a fault?

You are here and
Here is also good
It is quantitative, your improvement
Measurable
And socially acceptable

Fuck your construct.
Life is what it is.
Fluid
Intangible in most cases
And usually not in any way socially acceptable
Not the kind of subjects you discuss
In pleasant company

I'm learning to love the fact my company isn't
pleasant
I'm learning to love the fact that when people see
me coming they turn away
I'm learning to love my shadow
And my sharp parts

With the serrated edges
My teeth aren't just bone
But words which edge off of my tongue like
The finest razor
Fine red line
No pain, then slow realization of
The fact you're bleeding out on your desk

By then, it's too late to apologize
Once the blood is split, done is done
And I wouldn't if I could, anyhow.
Because, I need my solitude
Social hangover
Fuck your societal construct.

I'm lewd,
I'm rude and I take up space
That should have been taken by someone who
Doesn't break rules, or eggs or
Insert your analogy here.
I am no analog.
I am full digital all up in your face
With HD picture
And all real, ever too bright, colors up in
Your eyeballs

And I may give you a migraine and make you sick but

At least I am being authentic and I feel a helluva lot better so

Fuck you
And your social construct.
Get out of my office before I find my razor.

But some days
My tongue turns on me.
I still don't know how to control it when it wags
And I cut myself
Fatal fucking blows to my everything
Ow, my everything

I set appropriate boundaries for
Everyone
But myself.

Two Letter Words

So

Let's see if i get this right
If i do not go to college
I will not be able to find a decent job
But, if my parents are middle class
And their income counts toward my financial aid
I am no longer eligible
But my parents were too poor when there was
enough time to save for college
So
Now
I
Languish

Or
At 18 I could marry
Or get pregnant
Or both
And become independent of my parents
Get all the aid I need
But then be called a whore
And too young to know better
And settle for the best guy I managed to find in my
18 years of life

Who wants to take care of me

Oh
B-dubs
That kind of man is co-dependent
Usually abusive
And will force me to submit
But damnit
At least
I'll have
My degree
While i lay
In the shallow grave
He dug for me.

We Sell Dreams

We sell dreams and

Manufacturer wants
We tell you what you want to hear
Then
In our best attempt
Give you those things

Sometimes those dreams are janky
Sometimes we think you deserve better dreams
Sometimes we scratch our heads and wonder
how
Someone so brilliant
Cannot see
Their own brilliance.

We murder hope by
Selling you your dreams
Encouraging you to go where
We think you belong but
What do we know?
We are mortal just as you are
And we couldn't possibly know what greatness
you are destined for

We manufacture dreams
And sell them to you
Wholesale
Market value
Then tell you that you must be mistaken
When the price is too great.

In Light of Screwtape

Who the fuck thought of the name Screwtape

it's like, the tape of the star who did the thing

with the other star

that they shouldn't have done

or maybe the restraint used between

two in a kink show

or maybe it's when the clear tape

gets turned about

when working on a project

what it does not bring to mind

the dogma of Christianity

or even a Vegas chapel

it brings to mind inappropriately named things like

glove compartments

or things from a bygone era

like a landline phone

or a fax machine

or a dog's lead

(you aren't leading the dog, he is leading you, and ideally it would be the other way around.)

Red Tent Sisterhood

I'm a fraud

maybe you haven't figured that out yet

but I assure you under no uncertain terms

I am a fraud.

I was a town boy growing up

and I hate sharing my feelings

I hate healing but I love how I feel when I have

and I love you all

good gods though,

if you knew I was really bad at being a girl

or being human in general

I think you'd probably think differently of me

and you wouldn't want me anywhere near
facilitation

and would probably gently, but kindly

show me the door.

Hold

Are you holding together?

Have you fallen apart yet, it's been 2 years.

2 years past the expiration date and here I am

still holding

things move slowly now,

one technocolor hookah induced dream after

another

then the still

then the calm

then the clusterfuck

back to calm

how am I to understand this

wrap my head around this?

Where there were six, there is now one

then 2

then 5

maybe someday 9

but now

just 2

and so quiet

and so calm

yet my head is a myriad of sound

a million voices screaming out how I should
behave
how I should act
just one that's me.
it says "stay the course, do not panic"
but those internal voices
become external irritants.
try to hold it together
do you even know what that means anymore
can you do anything other than
stare
straight ahead
into the abyss which stares into you
and tell yourself
that what you did was right
when inside it feels wrong
how
small
u
feel

.

you are being punished for a crime that is not
yours
and that you turned in the perpetrator of
and you are hellbent to get back what you lost

yet hellbent to believe what you did
POWERFUL
they say
do they even
know
how
small
u
feel
?

Could anyone really understand what
it's like to lose your three children?
they aren't dead, but might as well be to you
no pictures
no calls
and yet
they can speak to the perpetrator
as though he'd done nothing wrong
he took HER innocence.
he took her dreams, her heart
he changed her into something she was never
meant to be
or maybe she was
maybe this was intended
the universe works

they keep saying
but
do
they
know
how
small
u
feel
?

Standing at the foot of a mountain
which no training
and you intend
to scale
the impossible
looking up, all that can be seen is rock
and tree
and sky
but you know you must
scale the mountain, or go as high as you can
until you can't breathe
until you choke on the clear thin air
and you cough out regrets
and your tears sting your eyes

and they all clap and say what an inspiration you
are but
do
they
know
how
small
u
feel
?

At your job
you fall behind
you wrench
you churn
you pull out your hair
you run
you hide
you do the best you can to keep up
but you cannot
the pressure is mounting
and you rise to the occasion
you take down almost all of your tasks
like a warrior
sword drawn
behind you

like a promise
and then they ask that one more thing
and you stand proud,
eyes glazed
head cocked
preparing to meet steel with steel
and you rush toward
the next unknown
assuring everyone you know what's going on
and you smile
and you breathe
and you take your sturdy steps
knowing full well the ground may cave
you feel your feet
and know your target
knowing full well what could happen
in a flash
then you strike
and that last task, that last ungainly foe
falls as though
it were made of stone
and you smile, but know that in the wings
lurks a larger, more unyielding
and everyone calls you a hero
but
do

they
know
how
small
u
feel
?

Apology

I'm sorry I can't come

to the phone right now

I'm broken beyond repair

You'll just have to answer

your own stupid questions for a while

whilst I melt down

and rebuilt in flame

i'm sorry I

can't come to your house right now

i'm still reeling from last week

and the aftershock of choices made

i'm sorry i

can't fix your life right now

i can't suck your dick

and make you feel better

because i don't feel well myself.

i'm sorry i'm a selfish bitch right now

i can't listen to your whining and complaining

about the constant litany of mistakes

that you keep making and undoing
til it is your own undoing

my heart feels as though
it is collapsing
under the weight of some terrible burden
still i feel vindicated
unalone and unafraid
but so alone and so afraid.

i'm sorry i can't live life right now
i just feel that maybe the burden is too great
great enough i can't pull myself from under its
weight

i'm sorry i
don't give a shit about the opinions you give me
this poem is not for you
this poem is for me

i'm sorry i interrupted you at your party
within the merriment of your finally perfected
happy bubble
comes my rainstorm
i really am sorry for that

i didn't mean to infringe on your real life
when you have one
on the rare times that you have one
just to rain holy terror down on you.
and have you dread again your monday.
stay home sunday
i'll take care of everything
just take care of everything
i'll tend the fires, you tend to you.

i'm sorry i
stained your carpet in my blood
let it run down the halls
as i ran for cover
screaming

i'm sorry i
never thought for a second
that you could be someone
who needed something
just kept taking and taking
giving away my only form of sanity

887749

You are etched onto my heart for eternity

I didn't say this was my choice
you are there, and you shall remain there
as you were, innocent, sweet and calm
not this monster you've become

You did not practice what you preached
the Nietzsche quote you spouted,
you became the monster you fought.
but long before anyone could
save you from your thoughts, which became
actions

You are etched onto my heart for eternity
I didn't say this was my choice
you are there, and you shall remain there
as you were, innocent, sweet and calm
not this monster you've become

You thought the perfect crime
no one would ever catch you
but then you became a braggart
and you were always a fraud

How to reconcile
These thoughts
For my feelings were always authentic
as I'm not smart enough to lie
I took care of you, painstakingly
and you took care not to alarm me, painstakingly
you took my daughter in my stead
you would have had her take your name someday
once I tired of your actions
you had your escape plan worked out
and I with no escape plan
ran around caterwaul
my best plan was a panicked plea
to a man to whom I once held favour
but my pain was just too heavy
and I wallowed for what seemed like an eternity

887749 is your name now
you have no name
you are not the man I loved
you are a monster, 887749
just like 887748 and 887750
monsters of variant degrees

You are etched onto my heart for eternity
I didn't say this was my choice
you are there, and you shall remain there
as you were, innocent, sweet and calm
not this monster you've become

…In the Time Before

Time

Head in your hands

no more use for crying.
You sit, the clock ticks.

Laying in your bed
No more time for lying
You lay, the clock stays

Remember who you are
Who you were?
Who you thought you'd be?
Are you really all that far off,
From everything you ought to be?

As you sit
The time clicks away as the water drains
There you stay
There's no way
You're coming out today.

What has come
What has gone
And all in between

What's the net worth of your desire over your dreams?
Through the cattle calls, through the persistent screams
Will you take up arms against that which binds you,
Or will you allow those critics within to childe you?

How?

How do I dare tell you that ship has sailed.

That you waited, procrastinated... then you were
there, then you weren't.
Its been 5 long years of my waiting and regretting,
and now here you are
and that ship has sailed.

I feel I should tell you
that I don't like the way you look at me.
as though I'm your last latest choice in
a myriad of others
who are better looking and better equipped
to deal with your bullshit

Slow Burn

You stand here

You tell me I'm doing something wrong.
You aren't me.

You may think
you know something I don't
you may think
you have something to prove

All you have proven to me is that you are
spineless, and lack a heart
Go ahead, challenge me to a battle of wits
Tie me into a ring
and we'll see who comes out

It won't be you.
Because I may not be brilliant,
but I am something you aren't.
And that is conscious.

Nostalgia

Memory makes the heart grow fonder
The earache doesn't seem as bad
The allergies
Being the only sibling without someone with her

How I cried for you
and you cried for someone else

It seems so much fonder now.
It was the central drama of my life then
but now, it seems like a fond memory
like a summer's breeze in the middle of January
But now you live it
and it's so humid your skin sticks to the seat

How I wanted you to be the knight
To sweep me away and off of my feet
But you were older and understood
That wasn't the way things worked.

The MAD Scientist

My insanity is complete now
On to the next phase
My insanity is complete now
On to the next phase
My insanity is complete now
I'm stuck
I'm on to my next phase.

Improvements

I've shaved a few minutes off of my
time
Running to work
Then back home

I only know my life is better with you in
it than without
I'm not sure it's your companionship
Or the comfort in
the lack of isolation

I've shaved a few minutes off of my
time
In running around in my own head

Fleeing thoughts
From the recoil of my dreams
Comes life again and again
Screeching to a proverbial halt.
and I in my proverbial press hat
writing the stories about the planes that
land.
Forever running circles around here.
For nothing, no one reads them

If I could just wrap my head around this
I know I would be better for it
I know if I could just explain
If not to you, myself
Today is Thursday.
Today is Sunday
They are all the same

I am like this every day that ends in
'day'
I'm still working
In this stress test of a job
They see nothing wrong with my heart
So they just push me and push me
Until the problem is made clear

I care too much
Or possibly too little

I shaved a few minutes off of my time
Answering the call
Helping the feeble and wretched

If I could just wrap my head around this
I know I would be better for it

I know if I could just explain
If not to you, myself
Today is Thursday.
Today is Sunday
They are all the same.

My heart broke this morning

9am
To the sound of the alarm
Amongst the dirty laundry
The whimpering of the white dog
and the piles of moving boxes.

My heart broke this morning
9am
While the world was all light
and the shadows even softened
To hear the sound of my heart
breaking.

My heart broke this morning
9am
As I started the car
and drove away
A tear in my eye
and a song in my heart.

I will get by
Somehow
I will get through this
Whether or not I am missing
By half, or fourth or eighth

I will get by
My world isn't ending
His is
Disconnected
Like the bill collector
Coming to repossess
The product intangible
But more precious than anything

Shutter

To smoke

to forget
to breathe to drink so alive
brown filter to cool water
brown water reflecting sky
Sigh.

Some to remember
some to forget
some to heal
some to mend

We are not separate
I feel your pain, you feel mine
You drink to forget.

The soft caress of long ago
and manifested into
a life you'll never know
never understand
and tortured yourself for many these years

To breathe in toxicity
to live life in breath
the clear air to smog
breathe it, breathe it

see this.
I am only this, a woman, nothing more.
I can create
I can destroy.
I choose to forget.
I choose not to heal
I choose pain.

Why?
Why do I want to live in this place?
The windows closed, the shutters locked,
no air, no smog, no light
shut up tight.

Shutter.
The world is cold
Closed.
Lie.

Who are you to say this is a lie?
Who do you think you are?
Why do I give you this power?
LEAVE THIS PLACE.
Like an unwanted and exorcised ghost.
Stop the phone ringing.
You can do nothing.
Just sit and be the powerless nothing you have
become.

You cannot enter my space if I do not allow it.
You break up my happy home
and think you possess the power to keep me
repressed.
Why do I bend an ear, why do I care?
You're nothing but an old witch wearing angel's
hair
white as blind on summers day.
just go away

Shutter
The world is cold
Let sleeping dogs lie.

The Future: Of Love and Razor Blades

Oh! I loved…

I loved springtime in the backyard

I loved watching your Uncle and your Father hide eggs for you

I loved, I loved, I loved

I loved watching the babbling brook;

More a tiny trench while I held you on the swing on the warm days

I loved, and I loved, and I loved.

I loved the way you mimicked every phrase you found silly

And I loved the way you brothers loved your sister

And I loved the way you loved your Grandparents

And your Uncles and Aunts

And how you loved to ask questions about the world

And how brilliant you were

How brilliant you are

We are in the future now, 4 years since you've seen my face

I am out here

And Oh, I love, I love I love.

You couldn't possibly know

How much I love

You

But someday, when you are old and grey, like me

You'll see all I gave up

So that you could be together and…

You'll see

That I loved, and I love, and I love

You

More than life itself.

A Tricycle in a Thrift Shop

Signifying a child who has grown into his 2 wheeler

But what if

It symbolizes instead an empty cradle

Child taken too early

Forever wondering

"Where is my Mother?"

Enlightenment

How Desperate for Enlightenment must one be to invest in used lightbulbs?

List for a Retreat

Four Cans of Spray Paint

Lavender Herb from Upstairs

Singing Bowl from Upstairs

Mexican Salt with Lemon from downstairs

Lemon Juice

The Sound of a Cello

The Breath of the Man Clapping One Hand

Forgiveness for Self from Upstairs

Forgiveness for Others Downstairs

An Angry Asterisk

Eighteen Small Mason Jars filled with the Remnants of White Chocolate from a Stranger's wedding, probably 2 years ago, judging from the smell.

The feeling of cleanliness

Semi-Permanent mud

Housing tied down with stakes

Something to wear that is red

But not REAL red

Just kind of red

Like maybe…

Collect rust from your car from high school

Flatten that out

And make it fabric

That really pops and,

When necessary

Inflicts Tetanus.

When I write

I do not write about you

I couldn't put it into words

It's like writing an homage to something

That is as old as the trees

Who so many have beloved over time

But when I do write about you

I write about nonsense

Because it is nonsense we both understand

How we are Intended

And how the bullshit of our lives aligned for one shining moment

And how when I first held you, you were home

And how when we first spoke, we were family

I lack the flowers to make that bouquet

How shall I put words to a feeling which has no words

The feeling of knowing that wherever you are

Is home

Where I can lift my feet

And sit down

And unload my day upon the air

And you listen

Either preparing the meal or just listening

To me speak

To the air

About some atrocities that have occurred in my presence.

Some as basic as being interrupted from my reverie.

Some as egregious as some sexist comment made to us

By some member of management

And you'll puff up your chest and say you'll handle it

But I know that it's a lie

And that's fine by me

Because home should not live in prison

I know what that looks and feels like

My blonde ones

Colored like the sun

And shining

And active

And running

Creative and flowing

Making movies, playing games

Programming

Making the world better by your presence.

But

Why so mean to each other?

Were you never taught that your siblings were

And are

The friends you'll hold forever?

Nevermind that now

Toast the bread

Spread the spread

And think about all the crazy things we aren't
going to do today,

Followed by all the crazy things we ARE actually going to do.

And I look forward to every adventure.

Because we have much to teach each other

Lilith

I have named you

It wasn't what your father wanted

We agreed we would call you Lily

Like the flower

Not like the person with the extra letters

I always knew

In my heart of hearts that

You would be the end of me

But I didn't understand until now that

The end is just another beginning

And you were the beginning of

Something amazing

You forced me to grow and change

And become who I needed to become to steer

A strong willed star seeker

Everything I did for others

Was an example for you to learn.

Everything I did for others, I did for you

I always knew you'd be

A force for good

And a force of nature

The name Lilith, which is your namesake, is you

Keeping mind of Satan

They used to say that a woman was needed

To look after a man

And now he's met his match

So watch out, world.

She's gonna change you with all that radical love
she found

She's gonna change you with all of that radical
compassion she has

She's not going to lay down silent while you beat
upon her

Or me

Or anyone she loves

For she knows the dark underbelly

She made friends with it in Pre-K

And now it's coming to put you in line.

Do not forget my lesson: live for now

Not for next week, or last week, but now

And don't be afraid to love a stranger

Keep your friends close

Your enemies behind a wall behind you

So that you don't have to look at them when they
finally give you the sword to take them down.

Stump

The holey stump which used to be

a symbol of my discontent

is now a symbol of the door way

I walked through to get here

and passing so many mirrors along the way

the shapes and sizes I could have been

the people I could have become

and yet

here I am

more deliberate

but ever me

you walk through the hole

and arrive at an archway

which leads to a meadow

with every color imaginable

and some you didn't see but recognize

as color, but sound

or light

Eulogy

Here lies me.

This isn't a trick

I'm not popping back up, this time.

I'm really down for the count.

Let it be known that I did everything I could to stay on that side of the dirt nap

You laugh, now, but really I did.

I've been having a fight with myself since I was in the third grade

About what side of the dirt I should really exist on

And yeah.

For the time I was there, I should have been there

But now I'm here

And I'm ok with that.

I hope I did everything I intended to do.

I doubt I did everything I intended to do

But I loved, and I loved,

And I fought, and I fought

And I did my best to protect you fuckers from yourselves but

Now you are on your own, suckers.

Be well

Be excellent

Be brave

Be flawless

And love

And love

And love

And love

And love and love

And love some more

Love until you can no longer breathe.

And you join me on this side of the dirt.

And look for me,

Because, if you've learned anything about me in these years

It is that I love veils

And no doubt

I'll be just on the other side of one

When you think of me

And smile

And laugh

And curse my name

Made in the USA
Middletown, DE
18 August 2017